PEARSON
PUBLISHING

Primary School History
for Key Stage 2

Roman Britain

Stewart Ross

Illustrations by Julie Beer and Lyndsay Crosbie

ISBN 1 85749 092 4

First edition 1993
Reprinted 1999
Text © Stewart Ross 1993

Published by Pearson Publishing, Chesterton Mill, French's Road, Cambridge CB4 3NP
Tel 01223 350555 Fax 01223 356484
Web site http://www.pearson.co.uk/education/

Contents

The Romans

Who were the Romans?

Long ago there was a **tribe** of people living in Italy known as the Latins. About 2750 years ago some of the Latins set up a city named Rome. Those who lived there were called Romans. In time the Romans became very powerful. They **conquered** all the tribes who lived near them. After about 400 years they ruled the whole of Italy.

The Roman Empire

The Romans went on to conquer lands outside Italy. By the time of the birth of Jesus Christ they ruled much of Europe and the **Middle East**. The area they governed is known as the **Roman Empire**.

The Romans were brilliant soldiers, organisers and builders. For a time no one could defeat their armies. Roman law helped keep order throughout the empire. The Romans built new cities with excellent roads running between them.

The Roman Empire at its largest

Something to do

Colour the map of the Roman Empire. Use an atlas to find the modern names of these Roman places: Britannia, Italia, Macedonia, Hispania, Athenae, Oceanus Germanicus.

The Britons

Britain before the Romans

The island of Britain (Britannia) was right at the edge of the Roman Empire. Can you see it on the map? Britain was one of the last places the Romans invaded. Before this, people from all over Europe had invaded Britain and settled there.

- The first settlers were hunters, who made simple tools out of stone and bone. We call this time the **Stone Age**.
- In about 4000 **BC** (BC is explained on page 5) farmers arrived. They set up villages and began to cut down the forests which covered much of the country.
- Some 2000 years later Britain was in the **Bronze Age**. This name comes from the soft metal (**bronze**) which people used for making tools, weapons, pots and jewelry.

Stonehenge, the finest monument of the Stone Age

Dates

We arrange dates from the time of the birth of Jesus Christ.

- Dates before this time are known as BC – **B**efore **C**hrist. They are counted *backwards*. So, for example, 2000 BC came after 3000 BC.
- Dates *after* the birth of Christ are known as AD. This comes from the **Latin** (the language of the Romans) words *Anno Domini*, meaning 'the year of our Lord'. AD dates are counted *forwards*. So 150 AD was before 250 AD. The year we are in now is an AD date.
- If we are not sure of a date, we write a small 'c' in front of it. The c stands for the Latin *circa*, meaning 'about'. So 'c 340 BC' means 'about 340 years before the birth of Christ'.

What can you remember?

Which was earlier:

1   1000 BC or 1100 BC?   _____

2   450 AD or 500 AD?   _____

3   100 BC or 100 AD?   _____

4   c 2300 BC or 2400 BC?   _____

Write the year we are in now as an AD/BC date _____

The Celts

The people called Celts probably first came to Britain in c 1000 BC – historians are not sure of the exact date. Celtic tribes **inhabited** Britain when the Romans first thought of invading the island. The Celts knew how to make things out of iron, so we call this time the **Iron Age**.

The Celts were a fierce lot, always fighting each other. Each tribe had its own territory ruled over by a king or chief. They built huge forts on the tops of hills. Today you can still see the outline of some of these hill-forts.

Celtic priests were known as **druids**. They believed they could control Nature by using magic and their special knowledge. The Celts were not just warriors. They were also very skilled at making beautiful objects such as the shield in the picture below.

A bronze Celtic shield

In touch with the Romans

The Celtic tribes in Britain were not cut off from the rest of Europe. For a long time Britons had traded with the **Continent**. Metal and slaves were **exported** from southern Britain. Traders **imported** wine, pottery and coins.

Between 58 and 50 BC the Romans conquered **Gaul** (the area we know as France). Now they were in even closer contact with Britain. Some British tribes made **alliances** with the Romans.

Why Britain?

The first Roman leader to come to Britain was Julius Caesar. He made two expeditions in 55 and 54 BC, but he did not conquer the country.

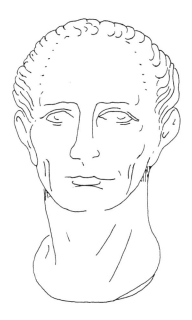

A carved head of Julius Caesar

The main invasion came in 43 AD, almost a **century** later. (Century is explained on page 8.)

There are several reasons why the Romans invaded Britain.

- Togodumnus and Caractacus, the leaders of the Catuvellaunian tribe, hated Rome. They defeated their neighbours the Atrebates, whose king fled to Rome. The Romans felt they should invade Britain to help him.
- The Roman emperor Claudius wanted to show his army that he was a great general. A good way of doing this was to conquer Britain.
- The Roman army in Germany was very large. Claudius wanted to cut down its numbers and keep it busy. He was afraid that the soldiers might make trouble if they had nothing to do.
- The Romans did not like having the warlike Britons just over the Channel. At any moment they might cause problems for the empire.

A carved head of the Emperor Claudius

Measuring Time

Centuries

The Romans remained in Britain from 43 AD to c 410 AD. That is almost four hundred years, or four **centuries**.

We measure the time each day in seconds, minutes and hours. 24 hours make a day. 365 days make a year. We call 100 years a century.

The first century *after* the birth of Jesus Christ (the first – 1st – century AD) began on 1 January 1 AD and ended on 31 December 100 AD.

The 2nd century AD went from 101 to 200, the 3rd century from 201 – 300. The first century before the birth of Jesus Christ (the 1st century BC) went from 100 BC to 1 BC – remember that BC dates go backwards! The second century BC went from 200 BC to 101 BC.

When it is clear what we are talking about, we do not need to write 'AD' for AD dates. But we nearly always write the letters 'BC' after BC dates.

What can you remember?

Fill in the gaps in these sentences with the right words from the following list:

tribes   conquered   century   Latin

Celts   Bronze Age   Stone Age

1 100 years is known as a _____.

2 In 43 AD Britain was inhabited by _____ of _____.

3 The Romans spoke the _____ language.

4 Before they came to Britain, the Romans _____ Gaul.

5 The _____ was immediately followed by the Iron Age.

Something to do

1 If there are 365 days in each year, can you work out how many days there are in a century? _____

2 When did the tenth century BC begin and end? _____ to _____

3 Give the dates of these AD centuries:

   a 5th century ____401____   to _____

   b 9th century _____   to _____

   c 17th century_____   to _____

   d 21st century_____   to _____

4 What century are we in now? _____

5 Imagine you are the Emperor Claudius thinking of invading Britain. In the space below, jot down the arguments for and against an invasion.

The Two Sides

The Roman army

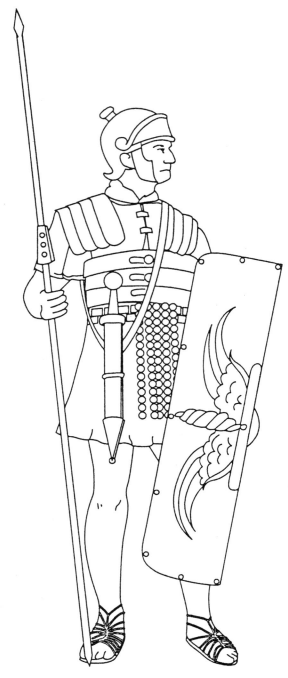

A Roman legionary

Something to do

Colour the picture of a Roman legionary and label these pieces of equipment: armour, belt, sword, spear, helmet, sandals.

The Roman army was the world's finest fighting force. It was in two parts:

1 **Auxiliaries**: cavalry and infantry from the empire's friends and **allies**. Auxiliaries had to stay in the army for 25 years. When they left they became members of the Roman Empire, or Roman citizens.

2 25-30 **legions** of about 5000 men each. A legion was divided into 10 **cohorts** of around 500 infantry and some cavalry. A cohort was made up of six centuries of 80 men each. A **centurion** commanded each century. **Legionaries** were Roman citizens from all over the empire. They were **professionals** (soldiering was their job), excellently equipped, well paid and carefully trained. Army discipline was very strict.

British warriors

British warriors were not as well organised as Roman soldiers. Although they **outnumbered** the Romans, the different tribes did not all fight together. The soldiers were not professional and many of them were not very well armed. Nevertheless, they fought bravely in battle and their chariots could be very dangerous. The Romans never managed to conquer the whole of Britain.

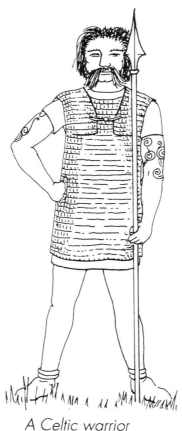

A Celtic warrior

Invasion

The legions arrive

The Romans invaded Britain in 43 AD with about 40 000 men. These included four legions. Their numbers were **II** (2), **IX** (9), **XIV** (14) and **XX** (20). To make these numbers the Romans used only three symbols: **I** = 1, **V** = 5, **X** = 10.

Something to do

Try to work out these Roman numbers:

III = _____, VI = _____, XVII = _____.

The commander was Aulus Plautius. He advanced from the Channel to the River Medway in Kent. Here he fought his first big battle. It lasted for two days. The Romans won after auxiliaries had swum across the river and helped the others over. Before long Togodumnus was killed and his brother Caractacus fled to Wales.

The map below shows you the route of the Roman advance.

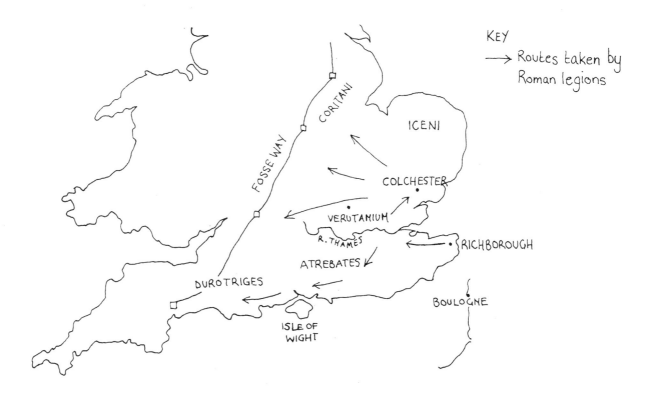

The Roman invasion and the Fosse Way frontier

The Emperor arrives

When Plautius reached the River Thames, he waited for the Emperor Claudius to arrive from the Continent. Claudius was in Britain for only 16 days. During that time his soldiers captured the **capital** city of Camulodunum, now called Colchester, and the British tribes in the south surrendered. The emperor was delighted.

After Claudius had gone, Plautius sent Legion IX to the north, Legion XIV to the north-west and Legion II to the south-west. Legion XX was kept behind at Colchester.

Soon afterwards the Romans set up a frontier right across Britain. It was defended by forts and marked by a road known today as the Fosse Way.

Something to do

Draw your own picture of the British tribes surrendering to the Emperor Claudius outside the ruins of Camulodunum.

Conquest

Boudicca

The Romans captured Caractacus in 51 AD. Nine years later (60 AD) Suetonius Paullinus had conquered Wales.

Then came news of a great rebellion. It was led by Boudicca, Queen of the Icenii, who had been badly treated by the Romans.

Her people rose up in fury and destroyed the Roman towns of Colchester, Londinium (London) and Verulamium (St Albans). Thousands of Romans were killed. But Boudicca's people could not defeat the Roman army. Paullinus returned and wiped out Boudicca's army. 80 000 Britons died and the queen **committed suicide**.

Boudicca

Into Scotland

Agricola was a governor of Roman Britain. 18 years after Boudicca's revolt he decided it was time to move the Roman frontier further north. He moved into Scotland with a large army, advancing slowly up the east coast and setting up forts as he went.

By 84 AD he was in the Scottish **Highlands**, where the warlike Caledonians lived. He destroyed the Caledonian army at the Battle of Mons Graupius, killing 10 000 of the enemy. He lost only 360 of his own men. Apart from the north of Scotland, the whole of Britain was now in Roman hands.

What can you remember?

1   How many men were there in a Roman legion? _____

2   What did a centurion command? _____

3   What was a professional Roman soldier called? _____

4   Give the Roman numbers of the legions which came to Britain in 43 AD

_____   _____   _____   _____.

5   Who commanded the Roman invasion of 43 AD? _____

6   Who was the emperor at this time? _____

7   Where did the invaders fight their first great battle? _____

8   Who led the revolt of 60 AD? _____

9   Where did the Romans defeat the Caledonians in 84 AD? _____

10 Who commanded the Romans in this battle? _____

2 The Roman Invasion

Something to do

1   On a separate piece of paper, draw your own picture of Boudicca's followers destroying the town of Londinium.

2   Draw a diagram to show how the Roman army was organised into legions, cohorts, and centuries. Say how many men there were in each section.

3   Write down as many reasons as you can find why the Romans were successful in their invasion of Britain:

_____

_____

_____

How do we know?

Sources

Britain was part of the Roman Empire from the time of the invasion to c 410 AD. How do we know about the history of this time?

We learn about all history from **sources**. A source is anything which tells us about the past. Sources are also called **evidence**. School pupils usually find out about history from things like books, packs and videos. These are made by **historians** – people who study history.

Types of source

There are two types of historical source

1 Original (or primary) sources

These come from the time we want to know about. For example, a description of Britain by the Roman writer Tacitus is an original source about Roman Britain, because he wrote it at the time. Original sources are the best way of finding out about the past.

A Roman lyre – a kind of harp

Something to do

What can you learn about Roman Britain by looking at the picture above?

_____

_____

2 Secondary sources

These are usually books written by people who have studied original sources. They are a quick and easy way of finding out about the past. Most of this book is a secondary source.

Something to do

1 Explain the difference between an original and a secondary source, using your own words: _____

_____

_____

2 Is a video about the Roman invasions an original source? yes/no

Original sources

Four types of original source about a **period** we want to know about are:
- writing such as newspapers, letters, diaries, poems or books
- paintings, drawings, carvings, photographs and films
- anything made, from pots and pans to temples or ships
- the spoken word, *either* recorded *or* said by people who were alive at the time

A Roman statue of a boy

Historians use sources like detectives. Sources are clues about the past. They put together all the clues they can find to build up a picture of the past.

Something to do

Look carefully at the list of four types of original sources given on page 18. Historians studying the Roman invasion cannot use one of these groups of source.

Write down which one you think that is (1, 2, 3, 4) _____ and say why you have given that answer:

_____

_____

Archaeology

Unfortunately, there are not that many Latin sources about Britain, and the Celts did not have a written language. Because of this, much of what we know about this time comes from the remains of objects and buildings found buried.

Roman clay containers found in an archaeological dig

Searching for this kind of evidence is known as **archaeology**. Some Roman remains, such as roads, are quite easy to find. But archaeologists come across other remains, such as the walls of buildings and pottery, only by careful digging.

3 Uncovering the past

Something to do

1 Which of the types of source mentioned in the list on page 18 do you think would be the most useful? _____

Why? _____

_____

2 In the space below, make a list of objects which

   a   last a long time when they are buried (such as bones or pottery)

   b   soon rot away in the ground (such as clothes).

Which list do you think archaeologists, are most interested in, a or b?_____

Why?

_____

_____

Town and Country

Province of the Empire

The Roman Empire was divided into provinces. Britain was one of these provinces.

From all corners of the Roman world came soldiers, travellers, merchants and **officials**. Some stayed a short time, others settled and made Britain their home.

In time the Roman way of life caught on among the wealthy Britons. They began to live like Roman citizens elsewhere in the empire. They started using Roman clothes and the Latin language. They worshipped the Roman gods and lived in houses built in the Roman style.

Of course, the old ways did not die out. But by 410 AD, when Britain was no longer part of the Roman Empire, the British way of life had changed a good deal.

Peace and riches

Celtic **society** was warlike. Roman society was more peaceful.

All over the empire Roman officials helped to keep the *Pax Romana* – Roman peace. The laws were carefully written down and those who broke them were severely punished.

Peace meant that the five million people living in Britain grew wealthier. Towns were built and merchants traded goods all over the empire. Britain's peacefulness and prosperity made it one of the most successful provinces in the whole empire.

A bar of lead made in Roman Britain

Towns

The Romans built Britain's first towns.

Unlike the Celtic hill-forts, they were sited on low ground. They soon became important places for meetings and trade. The streets were arranged in grids. In the middle there was a large square, called the **forum**. It was used as a market place and for meetings. It had shops and offices on three sides and government offices on the other side.

There were temples where the Roman gods were worshipped. Some towns had public baths, an open-air theatre and huge **monumental** arches.

By the 3rd century AD most towns were surrounded by stone walls.

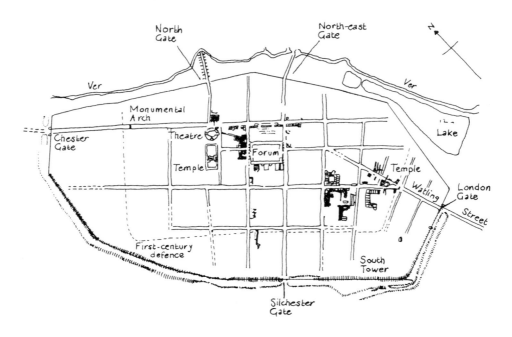

A plan of the Roman town of Verulamium, now St Albans

Villas

Most people lived in the countryside in small wooden houses, as they had before the Romans arrived.

Some town houses were made of brick or stone, with tiled roofs. The richest people built large Roman-style country houses known as **villas**. Villas were like long bungalows, spread out over a large area.

The buildings and walls **enclosed** gardens. The walls were decorated with tiles and **mosaics**. These are pictures made up of small pieces of coloured glass or stone. Some houses were kept warm in winter by hot air under the floors. Because they were made of stone or brick, archaeologists have found the remains of many villas all over the southern half of Britain.

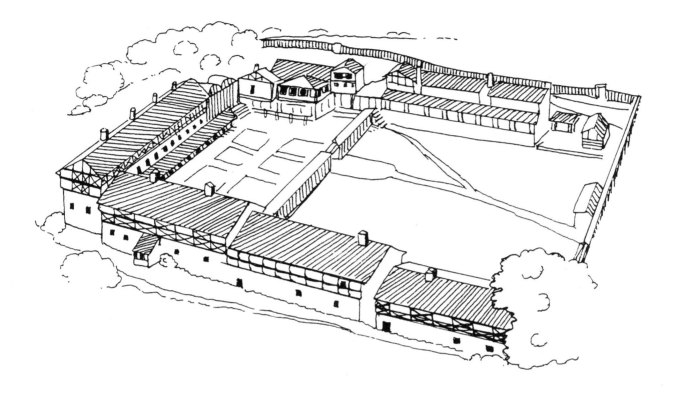

How the Roman villa at Chedworth might have looked

What can you remember?

Fill in the gaps in these sentences with the right words from the following list:

officials   archaeologists   forum   villas   mosaics
remains

1 Roman _____ helped with the government.

2 Villas were decorated with _____ .

3 Roman towns had a _____ in the middle.

4 _____ have found the _____ of many Roman

_____ in southern Britain.

Everyday Life

Roman clothes

The most famous Roman article of clothing was the **toga**, a long piece of cloth wrapped round the body. It was not suited to English weather. The wealthiest Britons wore togas only on special occasions.

Most of the time people wore tunics, with a belt round the waist. Over this they wore a cloak, sometimes with a hood to keep out the rain and wind. They wore sandals or heavy boots on their feet.

The Celts loved bright colours such as reds, yellows and blues. Their tunics were very colourful. Women and men wore heavy jewelry.

Women and children

We do not know much about women and children in Roman Britain.

Women were important in Celtic society. We saw, for example, that the Icenii accepted Boudicca as their queen. But women were not so well treated in the Roman Empire. The Romans would never have dreamed of having a woman as emperor. Because of Celtic ideas, perhaps women were better off in Britain than in some other parts of the empire.

Only the children of wealthy parents went to school. There they learned to read and write Latin. Other children had to work as soon as they were old enough.

Slaves

All over the Roman Empire much of the hard and dirty work was done by slaves.

The Celts had slaves too. Slaves were men, women or children owned by other people. Their masters could make them do whatever they wanted, and they were not paid for their work. Slaves who misbehaved or tried to run away were punished very severely.

Of course, not all slave owners were cruel. Household slaves often had quite a good time. But life was very hard for slaves who worked in mines or rowed the huge Roman boats (known as **galleys**). Sometimes fortunate slaves were given their freedom.

Religion

From a mosaic picture of Europa and the god Jupiter

This picture comes from a mosaic found in a Roman villa at Lullingstone in Kent. It shows the Roman god Jupiter changed into a bull. He is carrying off the beautiful woman Europa. The Romans had many gods and goddesses. Each one was in charge of a different part of life.

Some of the better-known ones are:

Jupiter king of the gods   **Minerva** goddess of intelligence and the arts

Mars god of war   **Diana** goddess of hunting and the moon

Venus goddess of love   **Ceres** goddess of farming

In some places a temple was built for just one god. A temple to all the gods was known as a **pantheon**.

The Romans made some of their emperors into gods. They also worshipped the spirit of the emperors (the **numen**). They believed that anything could have a guardian spirit, known as its **genius**. In many places the old Celtic gods and goddesses were worshipped as well as the Roman ones.

Religion in Roman Britain was pretty complicated, wasn't it?

Change and Continuity

What were you like?

Imagine 200 years from now, when you are no longer alive.

Someone is wondering what you were *like*. What do they mean? Do they mean you at the age of ten, twenty, fifty, or seventy? Some things remain the same all your life. We call this **continuity**. For example, you have the same name and you look roughly the same.

But other things change. You are not exactly the same now as you were when you were four, are you? You wear different clothes, you have different ideas and you are bigger.

In other words, although some of you does not change, other parts of you are always changing.

What was Roman Britain like?

Like a person, there was change and continuity in the **civilisation** of Roman Britain.

Britain was not always peaceful, for example. It had to fight off attacks of **barbarians** (the Roman name for people living outside the empire). But generally Roman times were quite peaceful compared with the times before and after. It is a useful **generalisation** to say life in Roman Britain was peaceful.

Most of what you are learning about Roman Britain is generalisation. Not all Roman Britons lived the same way, and their civilisation was always changing.

Change

During the 350 years that Britain was part of the Roman Empire, one of the biggest changes took place in religion. For a long time the Romans **persecuted** Christians. Then in 312 AD the Emperor Constantine was **converted** to Christianity. After this Christianity spread rapidly all over the empire.

The old religions survived too. So religion in Roman Britain became even more complicated!

A Roman head of Christ, made of mosaic

What can you remember?

Read these sentences and put a tick (✔) against those which are true:

1 Not much changed while Britain was part of the Roman Empire. ☐

2 Jupiter was the king of the gods. ☐

3 In Roman Britain most children went to school. ☐

4 The Roman Empire was Christian in 150 AD. ☐

5 Celtic clothing was brightly coloured. ☐

6 Children could not be slaves. ☐

7 Continuity means continuing in the same way. ☐

Something to do

1 Colour and label the picture of a Roman villa on page 23.

2 Make your own mosaic picture of a Roman soldier or villa. Stick small pieces of coloured paper onto a plain background. It is easier if you first draw an outline of the picture on the background.

3 Explain in a sentence or two of your own why religion was so complicated in Roman Britain:

_____

_____

_____

_____

4 Colour the map of Roman Britain below. Underline six Roman towns which are still important today.

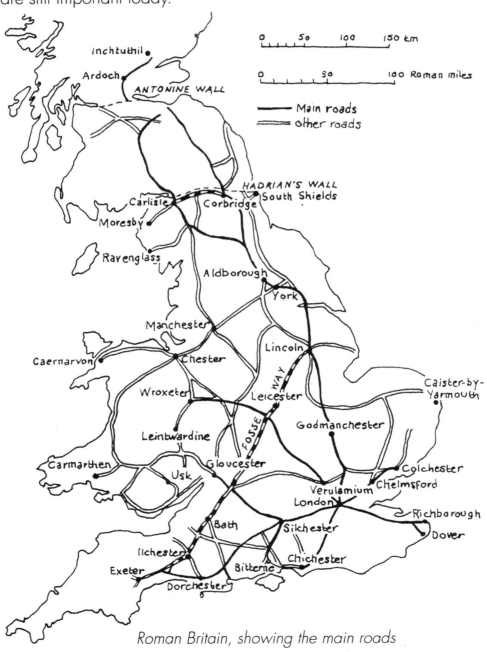

Roman Britain, showing the main roads

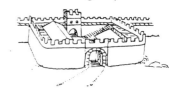

Britain Alone

The legions withdraw

The barbarian tribes living outside the empire were nearly always attacking the Roman frontiers. They wanted to **plunder** Roman wealth. For hundreds of years the Roman armies managed to hold off these attacks. But during the fourth century the empire began to fall apart.

In 367 barbarians invaded northern Britain and were driven off. More serious attacks came in 398 and 408. By the time of the last invasion, the Roman legions had been withdrawn from the island to defend other parts of the empire. They never returned. The British had to look after themselves as best they could.

One country

Before the arrival of the Roman legions, the British lived in scattered tribes. They were loyal to their local chief and their own people, not to the whole country. One of the most important things the Romans did was to give England one government. It did not last, but they had shown that the southern part of our island could be a single country.

What was left?

The Roman way of life survived for a while. In time, however, very little of it was left.

Today it is not obvious that Britain was ever part of the Roman Empire. We do not speak Latin or wear togas, and the fine Roman buildings have long since been destroyed. But Roman Britain did not vanish without trace.

What we have left from that time we call a **legacy**.

Roads and Ruins

Roads

The Romans built a fine network of roads all over southern Britain. They were straight and sometimes paved in stone. In one or two places the original roads can still be seen.

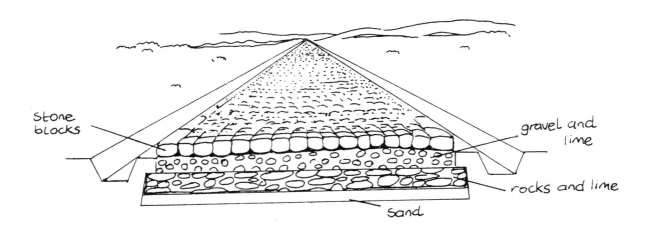

Labels: stone blocks · gravel and lime · rocks and lime · sand

How a paved Roman road was built

Several Roman roads are in use today. They are wider and covered in tar, but they still follow the route chosen by the Romans. For example, the Roman Watling Street is now the A5 main road.

In other places archaeologists have uncovered the remains of Roman buildings. Only the lowest parts of the walls are left. From these we can work out what Roman temples, theatres, baths and villas looked like.

Hadrian's Wall

The most famous building left from Roman times is Hadrian's Wall. The Romans did not occupy Scotland for long. Several times their legions moved there, but they always returned south again.

To prevent Scottish tribes from attacking England, the Romans built two walls across the country. The Antonine Wall, in Scotland, was made of earth and wood. Hadrian's Wall, further south, was built of stone, and was protected by ditches and forts. It is called Hadrian's Wall after the Roman general who ordered it to be built. Much of the wall is still standing. Thousands of people visit it each year. You can see where the walls are on the map on page 28.

One of the forts on Hadrian's Wall

Towns

Most Roman towns were built near Celtic settlements. These settlements became more important than others. Some Roman towns, such as Manchester, Bath and Exeter, are still important now. And the Roman capital city, London, remains the capital today.

Forty of our place-names come from Roman times. Chester is the most obvious – it comes from the Latin word *castra*, meaning a 'camp'.

Language and Faith

Latin

Many English words come from Latin. But most of them are taken from the French spoken by the Normans, who invaded Britain in 1066. Some of the few words that did come to Britain with the Romans are:

English word	Latin word
fish	*piscis*
wine	*vinum*
arm	*armus*

Christianity

Christianity survived in some places. The Romans have influenced our lives in all sorts of other ways, too. For example, Latin is still taught in some British schools and our month 'July' comes from the Roman general *Julius Caesar*.

But these things are the legacy of the Roman Empire in Europe, rather than Roman Britain.

What can you remember?

Fill in the gaps in these sentences with the right words from the following list:

Latin   Hadrian's Wall   *castra*   capital

1 _____ is the most famous Roman remain in this country.

2 The _____ word for a camp is _____.

3 London was the _____ city of Roman Britain.

Something to do

1 Colour and label the picture of the head of Christ on page 27. Remember that it is a mosaic.

2 Explain why the barbarians wanted to plunder the Roman Empire:

_____

_____

_____

Answers
Note: Children may need help with the words in bold type.
Page 5: 1 = 1100 BC, 2 = 450 AD, 3 = 100 BC, 4 = 2400 BC. Page 9, What can you remember?: 1 = century, 2 = tribes, Celts, 3 = Latin, 4 = conquered, 5 = Bronze Age; Something to do: 1 = 36500, 2 = 901, 1000, 3a = 500, b = 801, 900, c = 1601, 1700, d = 2001, 2100, 4 = 20th. Page 12: 3, 6, 17. Page 15: 1 = 5000, 2 = century, 3 = legionary, 4 = II, IX, XIV and XX, 5 = Aulus Plautius, 6 = Claudius, 7 = River Medway, 8 = Boudicca, 9 = Mons Graupius, 10 = Agricola. Page 18: 2 No. Page 19: 4. Page 20: 1 = writing is most useful, 2 a. Page 23: 1 = officials, 2 = mosaics, 3 = forum, 4 = archaeologists, remains, villas. Page 27: 2, 5 and 7. Page 32: 1 = Hadrian's Wall, 2 = Latin, castra, 3 = capital.